THE PRINCIPAL IS MISSING

THE PRINCIPAL IS MISSING
SCHOOL OF MAGIC™ BOOK ONE

SIENNA LAWSON

I dedicate this book to my mom and dad and Michael because they are funny, nice, kind and sweet.
— Sienna

Thanks to the Principal Is Missing JIT Team

Danika Fedeli
Kelly O'Donnell
John Ashmore
Mary Morris
Daniel Weigert
Micky Cocker

SCHOOL OF MAGIC

CHAPTER ONE

Callie looked in the mirror. Her bright pink hair was fluffy like cotton candy and needed to be brushed, but Callie didn't feel like doing it.

What fun was the summer break if you had to do boring stuff like brush your hair? Callie yawned.

Callie's dog Buster walked over to her. Buster wasn't just any dog, though. He was Callie's *familiar*, which meant she could talk to him.

"Do *you* think I have to brush my hair?" Callie asked.

No, Buster said. *We dogs never brush our hair.*

"That's because people brush it for you," Callie said, patting Buster's tan fur.

Maybe you should make another person brush your hair.

Callie shook her head and crossed her arms. "I'm going to be in fourth grade, Buster. Fourth graders *don't* let people brush their hair. I'm too old for that."

Maybe when Callie learned magic, she could use magic to brush her hair. Her mom used her magic to brush the twins' hair, so it made sense that Callie would be able to do it.

Callie got dressed and slid into the kitchen.

The smell of bacon and pancakes filled the air, and her belly growled. Her mom was flipping pancakes. She could've easily made the pancakes with magic, but sometimes Callie's mom liked to make food the old-fashioned way.

Callie's baby brother Harry and sister Holly, who were twins, were being fed by a floating spoon, and her mom's familiar, a black cat named Mr. Moon, lapped milk from a bowl on the table. "Good morning, Mom!" Callie exclaimed.

"Good morning, little princess," Mom said.

"Don't call me 'little princess,'" Callie argued. "I'm a big girl! I'm *ten* now!"

"I know, but you'll always be my little princess."

Callie put her hands on her hips.

"I thought you liked princesses," Mom said.

"I *do*," Callie replied, "But I'm not a *little* princess. I'm a big princess! Or a witch princess!"

"I'm your mom. Can't I call you my little princess? No one else has to?"

Callie rolled her eyes. "I guess so, Mom, but no one else can."

Mom laughed. "That's fair."

"Where's Dad?" Callie asked, looking around.

Her dad was normally the first in line for breakfast. He liked to steal bacon from the pan when Callie's mom wasn't looking.

"He's on the phone," Mom replied, "With another researcher. They're talking about how to hatch some Yuanat eggs they found."

"Wow, that's cool!" Callie exclaimed. "Wait, what's a Yuanat?"

"It's a very rare reptile that lives in Cuba."

"Cool!"

Callie sat down at the table and waited for breakfast. She watched her mom's brown ponytail swing as she cooked. Someday, Callie wanted to have long, straight hair. Curly hair just wasn't as pretty, although it was pretty cool.

Buster stuck his head around the table and licked up Harry's food. "Buster, stop eating Harry's breakfast!" Callie told Buster off.

"I'm not. This is my food," Buster replied as he crunched down on his dry food.

"Mom, Harry's eating Buster's food again!" Callie laughed, but her mom didn't think it was funny.

With a flick of her wrist, Buster's food was back in Buster's bowl, and Harry looked as if he were ready to cry. Callie's mom waved her arm, and a plate filled with pancakes and bacon floated to the table. A fork and a glass of orange juice followed.

That stopped Harry's tears, and he kept eating like nothing had happened.

"It's so cool that you can do that," Callie exclaimed. "Do you think *I'll* be able to do that someday?"

More plates of food floated onto the table. "Of course, dear," Mom said. "It just takes a little time and practice."

Callie's mom sat at the table and took a bite of the yummy pancakes. Callie did too, enjoying the sweet maple syrup.

Dad, a tall man with dark hair, walked in and sat beside Callie's mom. "Sorry to keep everyone waiting."

Dad's familiar, Twig, a stick insect, sat on his shoulder and chewed on a large, green leaf.

"Well, I suppose if it was for the Yuanat, it's fine," Mom teased.

Dad smiled.

"I want to see a Yuanat someday," Callie said.

Because Callie's parents were animal researchers, they often went on research trips, but Callie hadn't seen a Yuanat on any of them.

"You will," Dad assured her. "Yuanat are very shy,

but I promise I'll take you to see one."

"Maybe next summer," Mom suggested.

"Have you told her yet?" Dad asked.

Mom shook her head and smiled. "I was waiting for you."

"Tell me what?" Callie asked. "Is there a surprise?"

"Well...there is a little surprise. I just wondered, are you excited for your first day at *magic* school?" Dad asked.

Callie gasped and clapped her hands. "Magic school! Really?"

Her dad nodded.

"I didn't think I would get in," Callie said. "I only learned to talk to Buster last week!"

"Your mom and I know," Dad replied, "But you still found your magic before fourth grade. That means you should go."

"But that means I'll have to leave Buster!"

In her excitement, Callie had almost forgotten that. She looked at Buster, who slowly wagged his tail. How could she stand to be away from Buster, her best friend? Maybe she shouldn't go.

It's okay, Buster said. *You'll still come home at the end of each day. You'll have so much fun at magic school that it won't even feel like a long time.*

That was true.

"But what about you?" Callie asked. "You won't be at magic school, so it will feel like a really long time to you!"

If you're happy, I'll be happy, Buster answered. *I know you have to go.*

"Thank you," Callie said.

"And Callie, even if you were going to mundane school, you wouldn't be able to take Buster to school," Callie's mom reminded her.

Callie had completely forgotten that, since being with Buster all day through the summer holidays had been so much fun. "True," Callie told them.

She smiled and gave Buster a piece of bacon. He quickly ate it.

"I'll be the greatest witch ever!" Callie declared. "And make a lot of new friends!"

"That's right," Mom said. "I made a lot of new friends at magic school too, and I'm still friends with some of them."

"I am, too," Dad added, "And I met your mom at magic school."

"Really?" Callie asked.

Mom nodded. "And this magic school is the best one there is."

"And because you're starting this semester, you'll get to meet a lot of students who are the same age as you, and a lot like you! New witches," Mom exclaimed.

"You'll be able to bring your friends home to spend the night, too," Dad added, "As long as it's okay with their parents."

Callie's face lit up. That sounded like a lot of fun. They could have sleepovers and practice their magic together, and she could show Buster to all her friends. This was going to be the best year ever!

CHAPTER TWO

Callie held her mom's and dad's hands tightly as they walked to the school of witchcraft. "I'm not nervous," Callie announced.

She really was, but she didn't want anyone to know.

Her mom laughed. "I'm glad, sweetie. You know, it seems like a long time before you become a full witch, but it'll pass so fast! Soon, you'll explore the twelve different powers and graduate as a witch!"

Callie tried to recall what the twelve powers were, but that was a lot to remember. For her, the most important power was Nature. To be in the coven like her parents, she had to master that one above the others.

"That's right!" Callie agreed. "The best witch ever!"

Mom smiled, and they walked a little more. Then, Callie's parents stopped. "Here we are!" Dad declared, spreading out his arms.

Callie wrinkled her nose. *There wasn't a school here!* It was just an empty patch of land surrounded by thick trees.

"Where's the school?" Callie asked.

"Right in front of you," Dad replied, smiling.

The school wasn't there!

"It's hidden by magic," Mom explained. "The school wants to make sure that only real witches can find it."

What did it mean that Callie couldn't see it?

"Can you see it?" Callie asked.

Her mom and dad nodded.

Callie bit her lip. She couldn't see it. Did that mean she wouldn't be accepted? Did it mean she wasn't going to be a real witch like her parents? Callie squeezed her parents' hands tighter. "I can't see it!" Callie exclaimed. "Mom! Dad! There's something wrong!"

Callie turned around and hugged her mom, who patted her head gently. "Sweetie, there's nothing wrong," Mom assured her, her voice soft and warm.

"Yes, there is! I can't see the school! Does that mean I can't go in?" Callie asked.

Tears formed in Callie's eyes, but because she was a big girl, she rubbed them away.

"No, Callie," her mom said, squeezing her. "Sometimes, it just takes a little time to see it. It took a little time for me, and it's okay to be nervous."

"I'm not nervous." Callie bit her lip. "Okay, I'm a *little* nervous."

"I was, too," Callie's mom told her.

"And so was I," Dad added. "Sometimes, new things are scary."

"And it's okay to be nervous. Do you know what really matters?"

"No," Callie said, shaking her head.

"What really matters," Mom said, "is that even though you're a little scared and a little nervous, you keep trying. Everyone is nervous sometimes."

"Even you and Dad?" Callie asked.

Mom nodded. "Even me and Dad. And that's fine, dear, as long as you keep trying and doing your best!"

Callie smiled. "That does make everything a little better," she said. "I think I'm ready now."

"That's my girl!" Dad exclaimed, pulling Callie into a hug.

"Now, just believe in yourself," Mom said, "And everything will be fine. You can do this."

Callie took a deep breath and turned around. She gasped.

The school appeared.

It looked like a castle from a fairy tale. Its tall, white towers seemed to reach the sky. There were other students running around in front of the school. Some of them were much older, but others looked like they were the same age as Callie.

"Better?" Mom asked.

"A little," Callie replied.

Her parents hugged her again. "Have a good day," Mom said.

"We'll pick you up here after school," Dad added.

"Okay," Callie agreed.

It did make her feel a little better to know that she'd see her parents at the end of the day.

After her parents said good-bye, Callie walked to the school. She realized some of the students were practicing magic of all kinds. One girl waved her arms and created a bunch of bright blue butterflies. Another girl danced and made snowflakes appear all around her. Those were the powers of Nature and Ice—two of the twelve main powers—and these students could use them already!

They could all do more magic than Callie, who looked behind her to see if her parents were still there.

They weren't. Callie huffed and put her hands on her hips. She was going to be brave, no matter what!

Callie walked toward the school, and the crowd of students became thicker. There were so many people! Callie looked around and wondered if anyone was as nervous as she was.

Then, Callie saw a girl her age dressed all in black. The girl had the longest, straightest, prettiest hair Callie had ever seen.

"Your hair is so pretty!" Callie exclaimed.

The girl had thick bangs and small brown eyes like a little mouse. She didn't look very excited to be at the magic school, and because she was all alone, Callie decided to try to be her friend.

"Thank you," the girl said. "I like your hair, too. The pink is really cool."

"I did it myself!" Callie declared. "It was supposed to be purple, but it turned out pink."

"It's different."

Callie held out her hand. "Hi, I'm Callie!"

The girl shook Callie's hand. "I'm Molly."

"That's a pretty name! Are you excited to be at magic school?

"I guess," Molly replied. "Are you?"

Callie thought about her answer. She wanted to say she was brave and excited, but you also weren't supposed to lie to your friends. And Callie really wanted to be Molly's friend.

"I'm a little nervous," Callie admitted, "But excited, too! And my parents said that's okay."

"Oh," Molly replied. "Well, I guess I'm a little nervous, too. I didn't like leaving my familiar at home."

"Oh? What is your familiar?" Callie asked. "Mine is a big dog named Buster!"

"I have a mouse called Squeaks!" Molly replied.

"Really?" Callie asked. "That's so cool. I can talk to mine because I'm in the Nature Coven!"

"Cool. I can, too! I've been able to talk to my familiar for months."

"Oh."

Callie bit her lip. "I've only been doing it for about a week. My magic came late."

"It happens," Molly said. "I know lots of people

who got their magic late, so don't worry! I know all about magic, so stick with me."

"Great!" Callie replied.

Magic school wouldn't be as scary if she had a friend.

"Let's go to the main hall," Molly said. "That's where the principal, Miss Connelly, is going to hold a speech to welcome everyone."

"That sounds like a good idea," Callie replied. "Do you know where it is?"

"Sure!" Molly replied. "I got here early, so I've already looked around."

Callie smiled and followed Molly into the school. This felt like the beginning of a great friendship!

CHAPTER THREE

Callie and Molly walked to the main hall. The school looked like a castle inside, too. The stone walls were lit by magical balls of light floating overhead. Callie craned her neck and looked up, amazed by the lights.

Someday, she would be able to make those to light her own house! The ceiling was high, too, and had cool paintings on them of the witches from the four covens.

There were a couple of kids just outside the hall, laughing loudly to one another.

One of them had created fire and was letting it bounce over people's heads and up in the chandelier hanging from the ceiling.

Another student was making bright blue roses with very sharp thorns grow up the wall. Callie knew it was rude to stare at people, but she couldn't help it. "Wow! They're really powerful," Callie whispered.

Molly nodded. "They are, but they're really mean," she said. "I tried talking to them earlier, and they told me to go away."

Callie put her hands on her hips and frowned. "That *is* really mean! They should apologize!"

Molly grasped Callie's arm. "Don't," Molly said. "You don't want to talk to them. Let's just go."

Callie really wanted to tell the other kids to be nice, but she also didn't want to make Molly sad. Callie sighed and decided to let it go.

After all, if the kids *were* really mean, they might not listen to her. Anyway, Callie knew the best idea was to go to a teacher about them.

Callie and Molly walked into the main hall, where all the new students were gathered.

The main hall was a large room with a wide stage and many seats, half of them already filled. Callie and Molly sat beside one another as close to the stage as they could. It was very loud in there with all the students talking to each other, and Callie had to lean very close to Molly in order to talk with her.

Finally, a tall woman in bright pink robes walked onto the stage. She had long, curly blonde hair, and a large, black crow sat on her right shoulder. "Is that the principal?" Callie asked.

"I don't think so," Molly replied. "I think she's just a teacher."

"Why do you think she's here?" Callie asked. "Wasn't the principal supposed to talk to us?"

"I think so," Molly said.

"It *was* supposed to be the principal," a girl sitting beside Molly said. "I wonder why the teacher is up there."

"Maybe the principal is sick?" a student suggested.

"Maybe she's running late?" someone else offered.

"But the principal wouldn't run late." Molly frowned. "The principal and teachers have to be in class on time! Especially on the first day of school."

"Do you think something is wrong?" Callie asked.

A sharp whistle cut through the air and everyone quieted, surprised by how loud the whistle had been. The teacher standing on the stage smiled and waved, and a microphone floated into her hand.

"Hello, everyone!" the teacher exclaimed. "I'm very happy to see you all here at the Magnificent School of Magic! I'm sure everyone is excited to be here, and we're excited to have you! I am Professor

Wilson, and I am pleased to welcome you all to our magic school."

"But where's the principal?" Molly whispered.

"Maybe she'll tell us," Callie whispered back.

"Now, we have a great year ahead of us!" the teacher continued. "This year, you will take twelve different classes taught by twelve different professors. You will take six classes this semester, and six next semester. These classes are going to teach you all how to obtain each of the twelve main powers—Nature, Earth, Air, Water, Ice, Smoke, Fire, Lava, Infernal, Death, Life, and Spirit."

"That's a lot to learn," Callie whispered.

Molly nodded. "I've actually heard of witches who learned more than the twelve main powers," Molly whispered.

"Really?" Callie asked. She wanted to know more, but they needed to listen to Professor Wilson.

"I'm sure you're all wondering why I'm here talking to you and not the principal," Professor Wilson continued. "Well, the principal is missing. You will have to find the principal as you attend all your classes. Even though the principal is missing, we want you to work very hard both on your classes and on finding her. And without anything further, you will now be taken to your classes. We look forward to working with you this semester!"

Professor Wilson spun, her pink robes billowing around her, and vanished in a burst of pink smoke.

"Wow!" Callie gasped, impressed by the display of magic.

"That's smoke," Molly said. "Very cool, isn't it?"

"Definitely," Callie replied. "I can't wait until I learn to do that! I wonder if you can change the color of the smoke you make."

"Probably," Molly replied.

A few more teachers arrived and began ushering students to their classrooms. Callie stayed close to

Molly, worried she might lose her new friend in the large crowd of excited fourth-graders.

"I wonder where the principal is?" Callie questioned.

"I was wondering that as well."

They thought for a while, but neither of them knew where the principal was.

"What were you saying before?" Callie asked. "You mentioned that some witches learn more than the main twelve powers? I didn't know that was possible."

Molly nodded again, her face very serious. "It's possible, but it's not really a good thing."

Callie had already been thinking about how cool it would be to have extra powers, and she deflated a bit at Molly's words. "Why not?" Callie asked. "Is it against the rules or something?"

"No," Molly replied, "but I've heard that those witches always turn out really bad. That's what my parents told me."

"Oh," Callie said.

"No witch should learn more than the main twelve powers. Not even the smartest witch should," Molly continued.

"Oh." Callie frowned. Even though the witches who learned more than the twelve powers were always bad, Callie still kind of wanted to learn more about those other powers. She'd always liked to learn.

As they walked into their classroom, Callie gasped. It was unlike any classroom she'd ever seen. The walls were stone, and the room was lit by magical torches with bright blue flames. Instead of desks, there were long tables. At the front of the room, the teacher stood.

Callie had gotten over her nervousness, but now it returned in full force. What if she wasn't very good at this class? What if the teacher didn't like her? Callie bounced her leg beneath the table. She really hoped this class went well.

CHAPTER FOUR

The teacher of the first class had wiry white hair, with tiny glasses stuck on the tip of her very puffy nose. Callie thought she looked a bit like a cloud, but she didn't say so.

The professor stopped by the desk of a boy who

had a mohawk. "Do you always have your hair like that?" she asked.

"Yes?"

"Well, next time you're in my class, I want you to flatten that mohawk," the professor said.

She waved her hand over the boy's hair, and his mohawk went flat.

"Welcome," the teacher said, pushing her glasses up her puffy nose. "I am Professor Puff, and I'm your teacher for this class."

Callie held in her laughter. The puffy professor's name was Professor Puff!

The teacher continued, "This class is Spells, and here you will learn spells that already exist as well as how to create your own."

Callie tried to think of what spells she might

want to create. It sounded really hard.

"The key to making a good spell is to rhyme," Professor Puff finished. "So give it a try. I'll be here to help you if you need it."

She had to make *rhymes*? Callie had never tried to rhyme anything before.

"That sounds really hard," Callie whispered to Molly.

"It might not be so bad," Molly replied. "Just pick words that are easy to rhyme."

The room was suddenly filled with rhymes as the students tried to create their own spells.

Some of them made really nice spells. Butterflies appeared, lights danced in the air, and some students even changed their hair color.

Callie smiled. She liked to change her hair color with magical potions, but the potions didn't always work quite right. It would be really cool if she could change her hair with spells, too! That might work even better.

But Callie didn't want to try her first spell on her hair. She might mess it up, and her pink hair was really nice even if it wasn't the color she'd meant for it to be. *What's something easy I could start with?* Callie wondered.

Molly had already tried a few spells and had

several butterflies flying around her head. Callie took a deep breath. "Butterflies are lots of fun, so make one that's..." Callie's voice trailed off.

"The color of the sun?" Molly offered.

"That's good," Callie replied. "Butterflies are lots of fun, so make one that's the color of the sun!"

The bright yellow butterfly flew around the room, and when it landed on another student's desk, it turned into a small black cat.

"Wait! Why did that happen?" Callie asked.

"Someone else must have cast a spell on it," Molly replied, her eyes wide.

The black cat leaped onto the teacher's desk, scattering all her papers and books on the floor. Callie gasped.

"No!" Professor Puff exclaimed, hurrying to grab her papers.

The boy who once had a very tall mohawk stood up and pointed at the cat. "Cat, who is very black! I need you to..." the boy's voice trailed off. "I need you to…um, turn back?"

The cat grew until it was nearly as big as Callie.

"Cat, who is very tall! I need you to be small!" Molly shouted.

The cat shrank back to the size of a kitten and meowed.

"Wow, that was great, Molly!" Callie exclaimed, clapping her hands.

"Thank you," Molly replied.

"It *was* good," the boy with the flattened mohawk said, looking a bit guilty.

"I'm just good at rhymes," Molly replied, pausing, "So much so that I do it at all times."

Callie laughed. "Okay. I've got this! Black cat, turn back..." Callie paused, trying to think of a good rhyme.

"Uh, attack rhymes. Would you turn?" the boy exclaimed.

The cat meowed and jumped onto the teacher's wooden desk, and then *the desk came to life!*

The desk banged into a student's desk, and it came to life, too. Callie and the other kids yelled in surprise.

Everything the desks and cat touched came to life! Soon, furniture, papers, torches, and the lights ran around the room, bringing to life everything in their paths.

"Really?" Professor Puff asked, raising her voice.

The boy with the flattened mohawk clapped his hands over his mouth. "I'm so sorry!" he exclaimed. "I didn't mean to!"

Professor Puff's face turned deep red, and she looked like steam was going to come out of her ears. She practically shook with anger. "You are lucky the principal is missing, young man!" the teacher snapped. "Look at this mess!"

Professor Puff frowned and waved her hand. Right away, all the objects in the room fell back into place, no longer alive.

"Whoever is interested in finding the principal should pay attention to what James's spell did today. An awfully horrific spell, but a solid piece of a clue. Good-bye now, students."

The teacher sank into her chair and waved for everyone to go.

"That was crazy!" Callie whispered as she walked out with Molly.

"I know, right?" the boy with the flattened mohawk replied, as he tried to bring his mohawk back up. Every time he did, it flopped back down.

"What's your name?" Callie asked.

"James," the boy replied. "What's yours?"

"I'm Callie, and this is Molly." Callie waved toward her friend.

"Oh," James said. "It's really nice to meet you!"

"You, too. I thought your spell was really neat." Callie grinned.

James smiled. "Thanks. But I didn't mean to do it. I'm just not very good at rhyming."

"Neither am I," Callie said. "Why don't we be friends?"

"Okay!" James replied. "That sounds great!"

The three new friends walked to their next class and began talking about the clue.

"I don't have any idea what it means," Molly said.

"Me neither," James replied.

Callie thought really hard about the clue. "I don't know either," she admitted, "But I'm sure if we keep thinking about it, we'll figure it out and find the principal!"

"You're very confident," Molly said doubtfully, "But I don't think it will be that easy. So many things could have happened to the principal. We'll need more than one clue, won't we?"

"Probably," James said.

"Maybe the principal was turned into a piece of furniture?" Callie guessed.

"I don't know," Molly answered.

Callie bit her lip and tried to think of all the possible things that clue could have meant. Callie had no idea what the clue could mean, or what it had to do with the principal's mysterious disappearance.

CHAPTER FIVE

Callie, Molly, and James were still walking to their next class when Callie noticed that James had gotten very quiet.

"What's wrong, James?" Callie asked.

"What do you mean?" James replied.

Callie shrugged. "You're just very quiet. That's all."

"Oh."

James's face turned as red as a tomato. "Well, I'm kind of embarrassed," he said, "after I ruined the last class with my terrible spell. I failed in front of everyone. What if that's all anyone remembers me as? 'The kid who messed up.'"

"I couldn't get the spell to work, and if you *hadn't*

brought the furniture to life, we wouldn't even have a clue," Callie pointed out, "So there's nothing to be embarrassed by. It was a good thing!"

"That's right," Molly said, "even if we don't know exactly what that clue means."

"I'm sure if all three of us keep trying, we'll figure it out, though!" Callie exclaimed.

James smiled and seemed to feel a little bit better, so the three students entered the classroom and sat at a table together.

Unlike their first class, which had wooden tables, this class had stone tables. The room was plain and dark, lit only by candles along the walls. "What class do you think this is?" Callie asked.

"I think it's Fire," Molly replied.

"Fire? Really?" Callie asked, her eyes darting to the candles around the room. "That's so cool!"

Fire was one of the twelve main powers, so Callie hadn't expected to learn about it so soon. It sounded really interesting, though, and she thought about how exciting it would be to light candles with magic. She could light her whole room all by herself!

The professor swept in. The man was spindly, and looked like a really strong gust of wind might blow him away. The professor wore long blue robes that were decorated with silver stars and moons.

"Hello!" he exclaimed, spreading his arms wide. "Welcome to my class. I am Professor Yovino, and today, we're going to learn to use Fire!"

The teacher called the roll and then passed everyone a small wax candle.

"We're going to begin with an easy spell. Although you'll soon be able to create fire without a chant, we're going to start with a chant because it will be easier for you to work with."

Callie nervously picked at the side of her candle. Fire sounded really scary. *What if I can't do it? What if I burn myself? What if I set something besides the candle on fire?* She gulped.

"Here is the chant," Professor Yovino said, "'Fire, fire, burning bright, light my way through the night.' Now say it with me."

"Fire, fire, burning bright, light my way through the night," the class repeated.

"Good job!" Professor Yovino exclaimed, clapping. "Now, I want you to chant and focus really hard on making fire appear. It might take a while, but keep trying!"

The chant was a rhyme, and it reminded Callie of how poorly she'd done in Spells when she'd needed to rhyme things.

Maybe she just wasn't very good at this, but then,

Callie thought about what might happen if she *never* learned magic. *I won't get to join the Nature Coven with my parents! I won't get to be a real witch! What if this is a mistake and I'm not supposed to be at magic school at all?*

Callie's classmates had already begun chanting to their candles. Only she remained quiet.

Callie took a deep breath and pictured fire, bright red, orange, and yellow. She thought of how warm fire was, and of the crackling noise it made in the fireplace.

"Fire, fire, burning bright, light my way through the night," Callie whispered.

Not even a spark appeared.

Callie glanced around the classroom. It didn't look like anyone else had managed to light their candles either, so maybe she wasn't doing so badly.

"Remember," Professor Yovino said as he walked between the desks, "It's very hard to do these things when you're a new witch, so don't be upset if you don't get it right away. It takes a lot of practice to make fire, and it's not uncommon for no one to make fire on the first day."

But how did Callie know if she was just normal and unable to create fire, or if she was really bad at it? Callie kept chanting to her candle. "Fire, fire, burning bright, light my way through the night."

Over and over.

They chanted for a long time, but no one seemed to be getting any closer to creating fire.

Even Molly, who had been really good in Spells, hadn't managed to make any. Callie stopped for a few seconds and thought about giving up. She knew she shouldn't, but she was so tired of chanting for nothing. She had known this would be hard, but she hadn't thought it would be *this* hard.

Callie sighed. She *had* to get this right. She had to! She took a deep breath and stared at her candle. "Fire, fire, burning bright, light my way through the night!" she chanted.

Still nothing.

Class was almost over, too, but there was no way Callie was giving up before she managed to make fire!

"Fire, fire, burning bright, light my way through the night!" she exclaimed a bit louder.

She pictured fire and held her candle more tightly. This time, she was going to get it. She just knew it! "Fire, fire, burning bright, light my way through the night!" she exclaimed.

There was a loud pop and Callie's candle lit.

"Wow!" James exclaimed.

For a few seconds, Callie stared at her candle and its tiny flickering flame in confusion. "I did it!" she yelled.

Professor Yovino gasped and strode to Callie's desk. "Well done!" he exclaimed. "My word!"

Callie smiled and felt her face glow with happiness.

"Callie, is it?" the teacher asked.

She nodded.

"Good job!" Professor Yovino told her, carefully picking up Callie's lit candle. "And right at the end of class. This, students, is a clue to finding the principal—Fire!"

Fire and living furniture? Callie frowned and tried to figure out what those two things might have to do with one another.

"Now," Professor Yovino directed, "You'll head to the main hall for lunch. Good job, everyone! I'll see you next class."

CHAPTER SIX

Callie, Molly, and James sat together at lunch. The main hall had been transformed and now held long tables, separated by covens.

Luckily, Callie and her new friends were all in

the same one. "So, what do you think it all means?" Molly asked. "Fire and living furniture?"

"Maybe we're supposed to set the furniture on fire?" James joked, laughing as he patted the table they were eating at.

Molly crossed her arms and blew her bangs out of her eyes. "I'm sure that's not what it means."

James shrugged. "You never know. I mean, it's magic. It's not like there are limits. It could be anything. Maybe we're supposed to make the fire come to life!"

Molly sighed and poked her chicken with a fork. "What do you think, Callie?"

"Hmm?"

Callie tilted her head to act like she was listening. In truth, Callie was busy looking at the massive fireplace across the hall. Red, gold, and orange flames leaped inside the fireplace, and it reminded Callie of the small fire she'd summoned. She dreamed of someday being able to make a fire that large. The thought was exciting and scary.

Even though her flame had been tiny, she was very proud of herself for making it.

"What do you think the clues mean?" Molly asked. "Furniture and fire?"

The flames leaped around the burning wood. Callie paused, then slowly left her chair.

"Callie?" Molly asked. "Where are you going? You have hardly eaten anything."

"I'll finish it for you." James stabbed Callie's fries and shoveled them into his mouth.

"Going to the fireplace," Callie replied.

"Why?" James asked.

Callie shrugged and walked toward the fireplace. The heat of the fire warmed her face.

Slowly, she sat on the stone floor and looked at the flames and the logs. Maybe the clue wasn't fire and furniture. Maybe the clue was fire and wood, which was what the furniture had been made of.

A glimmer of red at the base of the fireplace caught Callie's eye. She hurried toward it and realized there was a small red box hidden there.

Carefully, she reached between the stones and grabbed the little box.

The teachers around the lunch room clapped. Professor Yovino was now standing beside Callie. "That's the next clue!"

The next clue? Callie gasped and opened the box.

Inside, there was a small piece of paper. "Feathers, scales, and fur, we caw, hiss, and purr. What are we?" Callie read.

"Chickens?" James suggested, walking to Callie and reading the note again. "Because they have feathers and scales on their legs, but they...don't have fur. Oops."

"Maybe it's three different animals?" Molly offered. "Birds, snakes, and cats? We're supposed to find those three animals?"

Before they could discuss the riddle more, a teacher announced that lunch was over and everyone had to go to their next class.

They had the History and Anatomy of Witches' Companions. When James heard the name, he groaned. "That's the most boring class there is!"

"No, it isn't," Molly replied, as they walked to their new class. "It's very interesting."

"On what planet?" James asked. "Nothing happens. The teacher just drones on and on about the anatomy and history of animals. Like where they come from, and what they like to eat. And what animal makes the best companion for certain types of spells. It's *so* boring."

"History and anatomy are interesting," Molly argued. "Especially if we're learning about cats somewhere in the middle."

The three of them took their seats on a long wooden bench.

"You're going to be an old cat lady someday," James said, "with like, twenty cats."

"I am not! I just think they're interesting," Molly retorted. "And even if you think some things are boring, that doesn't mean you don't need to learn them."

The professor arrived. It was the woman in the pink robes who had welcomed them instead of the principal—Professor Wilson.

Callie perked up when she saw her and the crow on her shoulder. She'd thought this teacher would be very fun and interesting.

"Hello, again! In case you have forgotten, I am Professor Wilson. I am here to teach you about familiars and their history and relationships with witches."

James groaned, and Molly rolled her eyes. "Be nice!" Molly hissed.

"But this is going to be so boring," James whispered.

Callie let her cheek rest in her hand. Professor Wilson's crow cawed from her shoulder. "Oh, yes," the professor continued with a laugh, "This is my familiar, Midnight. He's going to help me teach the class this semester."

Professor Wilson started talking about different

types of animals and what they were like. Callie already knew a lot about animals and where they lived because her parents were animal researchers, but still, the class did seem to be very, very boring.

Maybe it was because they weren't doing anything exciting.

In her other classes Callie had cast spells and created fire, but in this class, they just sat and listened. James kept tapping on the table, and even Molly, who had been so interested in the class, had slumped in her seat.

Callie hid a yawn behind her hand. It would be really awful if she fell asleep, but this class was so boring that she couldn't help it. When would it end? The other classes had seemed to go by so quickly, but this one was taking forever. Callie sighed and thought about Buster at home. This class would be much more interesting if he'd been allowed to come, too.

Finally, the teacher stopped talking. "Well, that's almost the end of class."

"Finally," James whispered. "I thought it would never end."

"That's rude," Molly whispered back, although she sounded eager for the class to end, too.

"I told you it would be boring, though," James shot back, "and it was."

"And I want to give you all the last hint," Professor Wilson finished. "If you want to find the principal, you need to go to the smartest room in the school!"

"The smartest room in the school?" Callie asked. "How can a room be smart?"

"I have no idea," James said. "Maybe it's a room that's alive or something? Do you think a whole room can be alive?"

"Maybe," Callie replied, wrinkling her nose.

One of the main twelve powers was Life, so maybe that power *could* make a room come to life. If so, what room would it be, though?

"This one is really hard," Callie said.

"Wait, no," Molly replied, grabbing their hands. "Come with me. I think I know where it is."

"Where?" James asked.

"I'll show you. Just trust me," Molly whispered. "If I say it someone might overhear, and then we won't get there first."

Callie shrugged. "Okay, Molly. Let's go!"

CHAPTER SEVEN

Molly held Callie and James's hands as they ran through the school. The three students dashed around corners and leaped over any furniture in their path.

"Don't run in the hallways!" a janitor yelled.

Molly didn't listen or slow down. Callie let herself be led along, even though she still had no idea where Molly was taking them.

Finally, Molly stopped in front of a room with giant wooden doors.

"What is it?" Callie asked.

"It's the library," Molly said, "The smartest room in the whole school!"

Suddenly, the clue made sense! "Wow, Molly," Callie said, "That was quick thinking! I would've never guessed the library!"

"Thank you," Molly replied, blushing. "Should we go in?"

Before anyone could touch the library's doors, they opened all by themselves. Callie walked in first. This school library was bigger than any library she'd seen in her life. There were shelves upon shelves of books, and some of them went all the way to the ceiling.

"Wow!" James exclaimed loudly.

"Hush," Molly hissed. "It's the library. You have to keep your voice down!"

James rolled his eyes and offered a quiet "Sorry."

They walked around looking at the books. After a few minutes of wandering, they found a tall old witch with her hair in a bun, wearing green and silver robes. "She must be the librarian," Molly whispered.

The librarian bent down to scoop a book off the table, and Callie gasped when she saw the furry animal hanging from a book shelf.

"What's that?" James asked.

"A sloth," Callie replied. "It's a really rare familiar! I've never seen one in person, but I've read a lot about them."

Actually, the librarian looked a bit like her sloth, and she moved slowly, too. Callie laughed.

"Shh," the librarian said, putting a finger over her lips. "It's a library."

"Sorry," Callie replied, her face warming in embarrassment. "We've come for the next clue to finding the principal."

The librarian's lips curved into a smile. "Welcome to the library. I'm Miss Alexander. Clues are to be found, not given, correct?" she asked.

"I guess," Callie admitted.

"So maybe you should look around," Miss Alexander said, waving an arm toward the bookshelves around them. "Books are full of knowledge."

That was true and made a lot of sense to Callie, so they all went to look at the books. There were so many of them that it would be impossible to read them all, and the librarian hadn't specified which books to look at.

Callie wasn't sure how long they'd been reading, but it felt like a really, really long time. Callie had a pile of books beside her that was as tall as she was.

James groaned and threw himself on the floor. "I'm dying of boredom!" he exclaimed.

Molly rolled her eyes. "Books are your best friends," she replied. "You should be more interested in reading, especially if you want to do well in class. You can't expect to pass if you don't read."

James huffed and crossed his arms. After a few minutes of lying on the floor, James got up and started walking cluelessly through the library.

Callie stopped reading for a second to watch him. Although she liked reading, she was beginning to feel a little tired, too. She had expected that finding the next clue would be hard, but it was taking forever.

Miss Alexander's sloth was swinging along the shelves, and James reached up and patted the sloth's fur.

Callie looked back at the book she held in her hands. As the daughter of two animal researchers, she really wanted to play with the sloth, too, but she also very much wanted to find the next clue before all the other students. With a sigh, she returned to reading about potion-making.

"I can't believe he's playing with the sloth instead of helping us," Molly whispered.

"Well, it *is* kind of boring," Callie admitted. "I can't really blame him."

"I guess," Molly replied, "But we're never going to find the next clue if we don't keep reading."

Molly closed the book in front of her and crossed her arms. For a few seconds, she and Callie watched James, who was trying to jump up and pet the sloth. The sloth didn't do much. It just slowly traversed the shelves.

Then the sloth stopped and pulled a book from the shelf. "Look out!" Callie exclaimed as the book fell.

James jumped and shouted in surprise when the book came down near his head. "Hey!" he exclaimed.

"Quiet!" Miss Alexander cut in, peeking around the shelf.

"But the sloth threw a book at me!" James protested.

Callie and Molly ran over.

"Are you okay?" Callie asked.

"I guess," James replied, his voice a little bit quieter, "But that was really rude! The sloth threw a book at me!"

"I know," Callie whispered. "We saw."

Molly bent down and picked up the heavy, brown book. "*Great Ways of Transformation,*" Molly read.

"Wait," James exclaimed. "Do you think that's the next clue?"

The students looked at the librarian, who grabbed her familiar from the shelf. "I wonder if it means something?" the librarian asked, smiling. "Do you think—You can take the book out, please return it when you are finished with it."

"It's the next clue!" James exclaimed. "I found the next clue!"

"Come on," Callie said. "Let's go out and see if we can figure out what it means!"

Callie, Molly, and James rushed out of the library, barely missing the crowd of their classmates barging in. They must have figured out the clue, too. "Oh, dear!" Miss Alexander exclaimed. "There's so many of you! Be quiet! Remember that you're in a library!"

Callie laughed as they managed to walk past the crowd. Soon, they were in an empty hallway, the rest of the witches having run into the library in search of the next clue. "We're a little bit ahead!" Callie exclaimed.

"Not too far ahead, though," Molly said, "And we still have to figure out what this book means."

"Well, at least we got there before everyone else did," James pointed out. "It'll be really hard to find the clue with so many people in there!"

"Right," Callie said. "So now we just have to figure out what this book means!"

CHAPTER EIGHT

The three of them sat on the cold stone floor.

Molly held the copy of *Great Ways of Transformation* and was making notes about it in a notebook.

"It *was* a really good thing that you found this,"

Molly said, glancing up from her notes. "Now, we just have to figure out what the clue means."

"But we're getting closer," James pointed out.

"Sure," Molly replied, shrugging, "but I don't feel like this book is very helpful. It's pretty good for explaining how to transform into things, but *we* can't transform into things, so we don't really need to know how. Not right now, anyway."

"Too bad," James said.

James tried to get his mohawk back. Although he'd been distracted by helping Callie and Molly find the next clue, it clearly still bothered him.

"Maybe the principal transformed into something?" Callie suggested.

"I thought about that," Molly said. "Only a great witch can master the art of transforming, and the principal is definitely a great witch. Even if we assume she transformed, though, we don't know what she became or where she is."

James agreed, "That *is* a problem."

"Is there maybe a way to figure it out?" Callie asked. "Is there some sort of magic we can use to find her?"

"Maybe if we were sixth-grade witches. I read the school books, and there are parts you need the teacher to help you with," Molly replied, sighing. "Right now, there isn't much we can do."

"You know so much about magic!" said James.

"Thanks," Molly replied. "I mostly just like to read about it, but I like learning, too. I wanted to learn about the four covens before I came here."

"Wait, I thought there were twelve covens," James said, "One for each of the twelve main powers."

"There are," Molly replied. "We learn all of them. But this school's focus is four covens: Nature, Fire, Air, and Water. I'm told that a lot of the older students are really competitive about it because we all have to share resources."

"Well, obviously, the Nature Coven is best!" James declared.

Molly sighed. "There isn't a *best* coven. All covens have their strengths and weaknesses."

"Really?" James asked. "But isn't the point to master all twelve of the main powers?"

"Yes," Molly replied. "However, you can only be really good at one. It's like how you can be good at math and reading, but you're usually a little bit better at one or the other. We're in Nature, which means that we're connected with animals and the world around us."

"Yuck math! But isn't that kind of the same as Earth?" James asked.

Molly shook her head. "Earth is mostly dirt and rocks, while Nature focuses on living things. There's also Air, which is the power to control the winds. Water and Ice are both powers that manipulate water, but in different forms."

"I want to learn to control ice," James said, spreading his arms out. "I could go ice skating whenever I wanted!"

Molly smiled. "If you really wanted to."

"What about the others?" Callie asked.

"Well, there's Smoke, which has to do with smoke, and of course, there's Fire. There's also Lava, which is like Fire, but it's fire under the earth. Like inside volcanoes. Then, there's Infernal."

"Sounds spooky," James said.

"It's kind of an odd coven," Molly admitted. "Infernal is sort of Lava and Death combined."

"Whoa! There's a Death Coven?" James asked.

Molly nodded. "They do a lot with ghosts."

"Huh," Callie said. "I bet they're great for Halloween parties!"

"Probably," Molly agreed. "Another power is Life. Members of the Life Coven make things grow. Pretty obvious. There's also Spirit, and that power is a bit like infernal. It's a combination of Life and Death. It's very rare to be in the Spirit Coven, and they're very respected."

"But not better than the Nature Coven," James insisted.

Molly rolled her eyes. "It's not about who's best."

"You mentioned that there are witches who master more than the twelve main powers," Callie recalled. "Since every power has its own coven, is there a secret thirteenth coven?"

"Well," Molly said, "There are rumors of a thirteenth coven—the Acid Coven—but I haven't found much information about it. No one seems to know if the Acid Coven even exists. It's like a ghost story."

"That's even spookier," James replied.

"But again," Molly continued, shifting uncomfortably. "All the witches who have mastered more than the main twelve powers have gone bad. No one person should be able to master that much power, so the less you know about it, the better. Probably."

"You know a lot, though," Callie said, seeing that her friend was uneasy. "Not about just the Acid Coven. About everything! I just can't believe how much you know! That's so cool."

"Well..." Molly's voice trailed off.

"But wait," James exclaimed. "What's the actual

point of the different covens? Is it just like a team you're on?"

"Kind of," Molly said. "Most people tend to get along best with their own coven simply because they have similar powers, but that isn't always the case. I'm sure if Callie here wanted to make friends with other covens she could. She's very friendly."

"Really?" Callie asked.

"Definitely!" Molly exclaimed. "I mean, you're very good at making friends. You're friends with James and me, after all, and we've only been here for a few hours."

"It's like your superpower," James agreed. "The power of friendship!"

Callie laughed, "Well, I wouldn't really say it's a superpower, but I do think the three of us make a pretty good team. Even though we don't know how to find the principal yet, we've done a good job at getting clues so far!"

"That's true," Molly said, tapping the book. "Now, if we can just figure out *what* the principal is, I think we'll have it."

Molly looked at her watch. "We're going to be late for class!" She sprang to her feet.

"What class is this anyway?" James asked as they headed down the hallway.

"Levitation Arts," Molly replied. "We're going to make things float."

"Really?" Callie exclaimed, thinking of how her mom liked to make the plates float to the kitchen table for breakfast. "How cool!"

Molly smiled. "It *is* really cool, isn't it?"

Callie nodded as they entered their next classroom.

CHAPTER NINE

Levitation Arts took place in a small classroom. There were several lanterns floating in the air above the students' heads.

Callie smiled brightly and fidgeted, eager to learn to make things float. "This is great! We figured out the new clue to finding the principal, *and* we're going to learn to make things float!"

"Sure," Molly whispered. "It's only a matter of time before all the other students figure out the next clue by getting hit with a book by the sloth."

"That's true," James replied. "But we've got a head start! That's a good thing!"

"Hello, class!" a voice behind them called.

Everyone turned around and gasped as the teacher, a short woman with long, curly hair and bright blue robes, drifted easily in and landed in front of the class. "Welcome to Levitation Arts!" she exclaimed. "Levitation, as you may have guessed, is the art of making objects float or fly."

She waved her hand, and the desks lifted a few inches off the floor. The students whispered in awe, and Callie sat a little straighter in her seat. She couldn't wait to be able to make things float like her mom could!

The desks lowered to the ground again.

"Now, I am Professor Blue. In order to master levitation, you must first learn to use the power of Air. This is a very fun, easy power, but it takes a lot of practice to learn to levitate yourself. As such, we must begin by learning to move small objects before you can work your way up. Today, we're going to create wind using a simple chant. Doesn't that sound exciting?"

The students cheered, and the teacher smiled.

"So here's the chant," the teacher said. "'Air, air, very light, move this thing in my sight.' Now say it with me."

"Air, air, very light, move this thing in my sight!" the class echoed.

"Very good," Professor Blue said. "Now, to move an object, you just have to look at it. You may not be able to actually move anything today, but your primary goal is to make wind."

James snorted. "Make wind," he whispered. "I'm good at making wind?"

Molly rolled her eyes and looked away, but Callie noticed a small smile on her face.

"Come on," James whispered. "That was a good joke."

"You may begin, students!" Professor Blue exclaimed.

Most of the students immediately began chanting.

"Can you take this a little more seriously?" Molly whispered.

"Why?" James asked. "What's wrong with having fun while you learn?"

"We're not here to have fun," Molly argued. "We're here to learn about magic, and having fun will be distracting."

"No," James replied. "You can have fun *and* learn. I even remember the chant. Air, air, very light, move this thing in my sight!"

Although James looked at Molly's notebook, nothing moved.

"Well, it takes practice," Callie said. "Air, air, very light, move this thing in my sight!"

Callie looked at the curtains in the room. They were light blue and made of a very thin fabric, but they didn't even flutter.

"I'm going to make wind!" James declared. "Air, air, very light, move this thing in my sight!"

Nothing happened.

Callie looked very hard at the curtains and tried chanting…over and over.

She thought a couple of times that she might not be able to do it, but then she remembered that she had made fire. Surely, she could make wind.

"Air, air, very light, move this thing in my sight!" James declared.

A cold gust of wind rushed past Callie, who jumped in surprise. The wind ruffled Professor Blue's hair and blew it into her face. The teacher laughed. "Good job!" she exclaimed.

"Nice job!" Callie told James.

"Thank you," James replied. "If there's one thing I know, it's hot air, right?"

Callie laughed then and redoubled her efforts. The air around her suddenly seemed warmer, and a gust of wind blew through the room and right into the curtains she'd been looking at!

Callie clapped her hands over her mouth. "I did it!" she exclaimed.

"Let's see if we can get the windchimes!" James declared, pointing to a collection of windchimes floating behind the teacher's desk.

"Air, air, very light, move this thing in my sight!" the students exclaimed.

The windchimes moved, filling the room with soft, tinkling music. James and Callie high-fived. "Go us!" James declared.

"Air, air, very light, move this thing in my sight!" Molly declared.

The book in front of Molly opened, the wind turning its pages. "I could read without my hands! How cool is that?"

"Very cool," Callie agreed.

Callie wondered if her mom would let her levitate the plates to the table for dinner! It would be really cool to show her parents and Buster what she'd learned.

Callie, Molly, and James tried to move as many objects as they could. They moved chimes, people's hair and robes, and the branches of a miniature weeping cherry tree sitting in a pot in the corner of the classroom. They tried moving heavier objects, like their desks, but the desks didn't budge even when all three of them tried at once. James tore a page from his notebook. "I've got a cool idea."

James showed Callie and Molly how to fold pieces of paper into paper airplanes, then they threw them into the air. "Air, air, very light, move this thing in my sight!" they chanted together.

Before the airplanes hit the ground, they flew up, caught by the students' magical wind.

The other students saw the paper airplanes and began folding them, too. Callie laughed as an airplane flew through the professor's hair and then upwards.

"Air is the *best* power we've learned about!" Callie declared.

Molly nodded. "It's pretty great," she said as she folded another airplane.

"And I finally got to put my paper airplane skills to good use!" James exclaimed. "I can't wait until I get home and can show my parents!"

"Very good job!" Professor Blue declared, clapping her hands. "I'm very proud of you all. You all showed that you understand how to master Air, and *wind* is the next clue to finding the principal! Good luck, students. I can't wait to see you next class!"

Wind? Callie frowned. *What kind of clue is that? It doesn't make any sense.*

CHAPTER TEN

After Levitation Arts, Callie, Molly, and James headed to their next class. They walked close together. After a while, Molly sighed. "I'll admit that I'm completely lost," she said. "I have no idea what wind has to do with any of the other clues."

"This will probably be the hardest one so far," Callie replied.

"Ugh." James groaned. "Why does it have to get harder? We still haven't figured out the *last* clue."

"And wind can be anywhere," Molly pointed out. "So that doesn't help us figure out where to find the principal. We can't look *everywhere!*"

"I'm sure they wouldn't give us a clue that makes us look everywhere," Callie said. "I'm sure it's supposed to be something smaller than everywhere, right? They wouldn't make it *that* hard."

"I would hope not," Molly replied.

They went into their next classroom for Basics to Advanced: Spells and Chanting. She hoped she didn't have to make her own chants, because she still wasn't very good at rhyming, and this class sounded super hard. It even had the word *advanced* in it.

"My mom told me about this class," Molly said, as she sat. "She said that my grandmother was the best of her generation in it. I really hope I can be almost that good."

"I'm sure you will be," Callie replied. "You've been good at everything else so far!"

"Thank you," Molly said, smiling.

"I just want to pass," James cut in. "That would be nice, but this chanting stuff sounds really hard."

"Hello, students!"

This professor was a very pretty woman with silver robes. "My name is Professor Lunes, but I prefer everyone call me by my first name, which is Ella. Like Cinder*ella*!"

The teacher strode to the front of the class and spread her arms wide. "Today, I'm going to teach you a spell that will help you unveil an object I've hidden in the classroom, but there's a catch,"

Professor Ella said. "The spell will only work if you know what the object you're looking for looks like. At the very least, you must know the name of the object. This, of course, makes the spell much more difficult."

Callie bit her lip. This sounded really hard, but she also really wanted to find the object. It seemed almost like a game, and games were fun! And she couldn't wait to tell her parents everything she had learned and about searching for the principal!

"Here's the spell," the teacher said. "'Object, object, hidden from sight, I ask you to come to light!' Say it with me!"

"Object, object, hidden from sight, I ask you to come to light!" Callie and her classmates chanted.

"Very good," Professor Ella said.

The professor smiled and sat on her desk. As she did, the class caught sight of her feet. On one foot she wore a shiny, silver slipper, but the other foot was bare.

"We're looking for your slipper!" Molly exclaimed.

Professor Ella laughed. "You're right, but that doesn't mean this will be easy. And remember, students, this *will* be on the test at the end of the semester!"

"Object, object, hidden from sight, I ask you to come to light!" Callie chanted.

The other students chanted, too.

They began turning in different directions, hoping to chant in the direction of the object and have an easier time finding it. James tried and accidentally bumped into Molly. "Oops! Sorry, Molly!"

"It's fine," Molly replied, her focus clearly on finding the silver slipper. "Object, object, hidden from sight, I ask you to come to light!"

To Callie, it looked like all the other students had already turned in all the directions, and yet they still hadn't found the silver slipper.

Callie wondered where it might be hidden when everyone was chanting and walking around the room. James had started waving his hands, too, like he hoped he might bump into the hidden object and find it without the spell.

Molly took to walking around the room, stopping every few feet to chant at another spot. She clearly wasn't going to miss an inch of the classroom. Callie stayed in her seat and frowned. Walking around didn't seem to help, anyway.

Professor Ella sat on her desk, swinging her feet. The single silver slipper shone in the classroom lights, and her other foot remained bare. Callie put her lips together, thinking. "Object, object, hidden from sight, I ask you to come to light!" Callie chanted.

Nothing happened.

Callie tried chanting at her desk, at the professor's desk, at everything in sight, but the silver slipper still didn't reveal itself. This was probably the hardest thing they'd been asked to do.

James was still waving his arms and staring at the ceiling. He bumped into another student and smiled a little guiltily as he returned to his seat. Molly had made it halfway across the room and still had no luck.

Callie sighed and looked at Professor Ella again. The professor smiled and arched an eyebrow. Callie looked down at the silver slipper and then at her professor's bare foot. "Object, object, hidden from sight, I ask you to come to light!" Callie chanted.

The air around the professor shone bright white, then there was a sharp, musical noise, and the silver slipper appeared on the professor's foot.

"Great job, Callie!" Professor Ella exclaimed.

"*Me?*" Callie asked in disbelief.

How did I find the slipper? Was Professor Ella right? Was it really me?

"Yes, you!" Professor Ella exclaimed.

Callie gasped. "It wasn't hidden at all! I was chanting at your bare foot. It's been there the whole time!"

Professor Ella laughed. "That's exactly right. Now, students, I will allow you to finish class early so you can find the principal. You must use what you've learned today to find the principal, and whoever finds the principal gets to be principal for a whole day!"

The students cheered.

"Hey, that's really cool," James whispered.

"I know!" Molly replied. "Think of all the great things you could do as principal!"

Callie tried to think about what she would do. So many people were trying to win that she doubted she would be the one to find the principal, and she wasn't as smart as Molly. If anyone could find the principal it was Molly, but Callie still really wanted to find her.

"Okay, guys!" Callie exclaimed. "It's time to find the principal!"

CHAPTER ELEVEN

Callie and her friends took to the halls with the rest of the students. It was a mess, with students running and chanting in every direction. Callie walked close to the wall for fear of having someone run into her.

"Object, object, hidden from sight, I ask you to come to light!" the students chanted.

Some students, as James had tried, waved their arms as they walked.

"The principal must be having so much fun seeing us all chanting around the school, thinking she's in the toilets and the attic like some of the kids," Molly said.

She jumped as a couple of students ran past her, shouting that they were going to check the bathrooms again.

Molly sighed. "They're all buzzing around like bees and flies!" she exclaimed. "It would be better for us to be organized. We can't just go around looking willy-nilly!"

James laughed. "But that's no fun!"

"It is, too, and it will be more fun once we find the principal," Molly replied, crossing her arms.

"Don't argue!" Callie cut in. "Let's just think a minute. What about our clues?"

Molly frowned. "You're right, Callie. Maybe we need to think back to the last clue, wind, and try and crack it. We never did figure out what it was supposed to mean."

"Maybe she's a paper airplane," James suggested. "That's what *I* would be."

"Object, object, hidden from sight, I ask you to come to light!"

Callie sighed. "It's hard to think with all the noise."

"I know," Molly said. "Ugh."

"Anyway, I need to use the bathroom," Callie said. "I'll be right back."

"We'll be right here," Molly replied, "trying to figure the clue out. Maybe we'll have an answer when you get back!"

Callie hoped so. She walked to the bathroom,

dodging around chanting and waving students. Molly was probably right; they should come up with a better plan. When Callie reached the bathroom and twisted the knob, it was locked.

She frowned. Well, surely, there was a bathroom on the second floor, too, right? Callie climbed the staircase to her left.

"Object, object, hidden from sight, I ask you to come to light!" students chanted, storming down the stairs.

Callie held tightly to the rail and inched up to the second floor. There were fourth grade students everywhere.

There were too many people crammed into a very small hallway, and she didn't like it.

"Object, object, hidden from sight, I ask you to come to light!"

The chanting students made their way to a staircase at the other end of the hall, going to the next floor. Seeing that most of them were leaving, Callie waited where she was.

Finally, she was alone. Callie sighed. Now, it was time to find a bathroom.

She looked around, peeking into rooms.

None of them looked like a bathroom.

Then, she felt wind blow through her hair. It was cool and pleasant, and wind was one of the clues. Callie frowned and followed the wind into a large office. It was filled with furniture and had a dark green carpet.

Above it, a massive crystal chandelier lit the air. "Wow," Callie whispered.

What was this place?

Suddenly, she realized that an office so big had to belong to the most powerful and important person in the school.

It was the principal's office! Callie gasped.

For a second, she wondered if she was allowed in there. Then, she realized that she might be able to find another clue in the room. After all, where better to look than in the woman's office?

The bathroom forgotten, Callie quickly looked at the principal's books and beneath her desk. "Object,

object, hidden from sight, I ask you to come to light!" she chanted to the bookcase.

Nothing.

"Object, object, hidden from sight, I ask you to come to light!" she chanted to the desk.

Still nothing.

Callie opened drawers and cabinets, finding only papers and more books. It looked like the principal really liked to read, which wasn't surprising. You would probably have to be very smart and read a lot to be a principal, especially of a magical school.

Wait. Hadn't Professor Ella said there wouldn't be any more clues?

Callie sighed. That meant she wasn't going to find anything in this room. That was too bad. With a frown, Callie leaned against the principal's desk and looked up at the ceiling—which wasn't normal. It was painted bright blue and had silver and gold stars that moved as Callie watched.

"Object, object, hidden from sight, I ask you to come to light!" Callie called to the ceiling.

Nothing happened.

Okay, so it wasn't the ceiling.

Callie looked up at the sparkling chandelier. Now that she really looked at it, she realized that the chandelier wasn't chained up or hanging from anything. It was floating in midair. Floating, levitation.

Callie walked away from the desk and stood directly beneath the chandelier. She stared very hard at it and tried to remember everything she'd learned so far in magic school today.

What were their clues? James made the furniture come to life. There was transformation, wind, and a spell about hiding things. Like Professor Ella's slipper. Only Professor Ella's slipper hadn't really been hidden. It had been in plain sight, right on her foot where you would put your shoe.

What was the chant I learned last class? It was the same one that all the students had been chanting as they walked through the school. "Object, object..."

She took a deep breath and looked up at the chandelier. "Object, object, hidden from sight, I ask you to come to light!"

The chandelier disappeared.

Callie gasped, worried for a second that she'd done the wrong thing, but a tall lady in green robes appeared. "Welcome!" the new arrival exclaimed. "You did it! I'm the principal!"

"Really?" Callie asked.

"Yes! And you found me! It was a smart hiding place, wasn't it? What other school can you go to that has a chandelier for a principal? Or is it a principal for a chandelier?"

Callie smiled at the joke, but she couldn't help but feel all warm and fuzzy inside. She had really found the principal, and she had found her before anyone else!

"Now," the principal said, "let's get you and the rest of your classmates to the main hall so we can give everyone the good news!"

CHAPTER TWELVE

The principal's office disappeared, and Callie blinked in surprise and stumbled a bit.

Once the room shifted into focus, she realized she stood in the main hall. Callie gasped and spun.

Professor Wilson was there and smiled brightly. "Congratulations!" she exclaimed. "I'm so happy you found the principal. I was worried I was going to have to take over for her forever! I would have been so tired."

Callie blushed. "Thank you."

"Now," Professor Wilson continued, "let's get your classmates back!"

The professor snapped her fingers, and Callie's classmates appeared around her. Callie picked nervously at her nails.

All her classmates were talking all around her. The room was very loud and hot, and Callie felt like everyone was staring at her. She thought of moving over to her friends.

Callie searched for Molly and James. They stood near her and looked curiously at her.

"Hello!" the principal exclaimed.

Callie turned around, and the principal smiled and patted her shoulder. "Great job!"

Callie smiled back. She felt a little less lonely and embarrassed with Miss Connelly beside her.

There was an awkward silence as Callie's classmates tried to figure out what exactly had happened. Callie smiled at James and Molly, who looked at one another.

"I am Principal Connelly!" the principal shouted, waving at everyone. "It is a pleasure to welcome you all to my magical school! This young witch beside me, Callie, was the first to find me!"

There was slow clapping, and Callie realized it was Molly. James clapped, too.

After a few seconds, all the students clapped and cheered. Callie felt her face get warm, but she smiled and let out a nervous little laugh. She had really done it! She had found the principal before anyone else!

After a little while, the principal waved her hands. "Now, now! Quiet down," she said. "We also need to tell Callie that she will be principal for a day! No, let's make it a week! Yes. Callie will be the principal for a whole week as a reward for finding me!"

The students cheered again, and Callie smiled, looking right at her friends. Without them, she wouldn't have found the principal at all! Maybe she didn't want to be principal if her friends, who had helped her, couldn't be principal too! That wasn't fair, and Callie wanted to be fair.

"Wait," Callie said. "Principal, if I'm the principal, can I make other people principals?"

The principal raised a very bushy white eyebrow. It moved—and Callie realized it was actually a fuzzy white caterpillar—then it disappeared. "Why would you want to make other people principals?" she asked. "*You* found me, and get to be principal as your reward."

"I know," Callie replied, "But I didn't find you all by myself. I found you because my friends Molly and James helped me find and figure out the clues."

The principal hummed. "Well, I suppose it can be allowed, if your friends helped you. Yes, that's very nice of you. They're lucky to have a friend like you."

Callie smiled and ran to her friends, then grabbed their hands and brought them to the center of the circle with her.

"Callie and her friends will *all* be principals of this school for a week!" Principal Connelly announced.

The students cheered and clapped again.

"Now," the principal said, "we must celebrate!"

With a sweep of her hand, the main hall was filled with music and lights. A table filled with all kinds of sweets—cookies, cupcakes, and candy—appeared.

"With a party!" the principal exclaimed.

Except for Callie and her friends, the kids all cheered and ran to the table of goodies.

"Good job once again," the principal said. "I can't wait to see what changes you three make to the school as principals for a week!"

Callie's face lit up as she thought of all the things she could do that would help make the school a better place. This would be really fun, especially if she had her friends to work with her.

"Have fun at the party," the principal said, disappearing into the crowd.

"Good job finding the principal!" James exclaimed. "And now we all get to be principals! This is going to be the best week ever!"

"Yes," Molly echoed. "Good job, Callie! I'm a little disappointed we weren't with you, though. That would have been really cool."

"Well, that's true," Callie said, "but without your help, I never would have found her! We all got the clues and we worked on them together, so in a way, we *did* all find her!"

"I guess that's true," Molly replied, smiling.

"We're much stronger together," Callie added, "because we're all good at different things, and that's why we're going to be such great principals!"

"That's right," Molly said. "We have a week to do whatever we want to make the school a better place! I'm going to make a list after school today of all the things I think we should improve."

"Well," James said, "I only want two things."

"Oh?" Callie asked.

"A skatepark," James replied.

"Oh, no," Molly said. "No skatepark. That would be loud, and take up so much room! And skateboarding is dangerous! Someone might get hurt!"

"Not if everyone wears their helmets and kneepads!" James argued.

Molly rolled her eyes. "What is the second thing you want?"

"To be allowed to wear my mohawk!" James exclaimed, waving his arms. "They keep making me flatten it, and that's not fair! I'm going to change the rules so I can have whatever hair I want!"

Callie and Molly laughed.

"Okay, we can change the hair rule," Molly agreed. "I think that's a good place to start."

"Of course, it is," James replied. "*I* thought of it."

"Okay, don't get *too* proud of that," Molly said. "That's just one idea, and we have to make choices all week. That's a lot of time to be principals of the whole school. This is a big responsibility."

Callie smiled. "It is, but guess what? We'll do the best job ever. And do you know why?"

"Because we have the best ideas?" James asked.

"Because there's three of us?"

"Not quite," Callie said, "Because we're best friends, that's why! If we all work together, there's no way we can fail!"

Molly and James smiled at her, and Callie smiled back. This was going to be the best week ever!

THE PRINCIPAL IS MISSING

SIENNA'S NOTES

WRITTEN OCTOBER 9, 2018

Hi, Sienna here,

Thank you for reading my book. I hope you enjoyed it as much as I enjoyed creating it!

Nine fun facts about me:

1. My name is Callie Sienna Lawson.
2. I had a dog called Buster.
3. I know some Spanish.
4. I love to sing and post videos on Tik Tok.
5. Pizza is my favorite food.
6. I love Manchester City Football Club.
7. I like to spend time with my family and friends.

SIENNA'S NOTES

8. I love my school. Go Coram!
9. I'm nine.

Off to ride my bike, bye for now.

--Sienna

CONNECT WITH SIENNA

Tik Tok:
@callielawson11176

Instagram:
https://www.instagram.com/callie_lawsonmcfc/

The Principal Is Missing (this book) is a work of fiction. All of the characters, organizations, and events portrayed in this novel are either products of the author's imagination or are used fictitiously. Sometimes both.

Copyright © 2018 Sienna Lawson
Cover by Tuire Siiriainen
Cover copyright © LMBPN Publishing

LMBPN Publishing supports the right to free expression and the value of copyright. The purpose of copyright is to encourage writers and artists to produce the creative works that enrich our culture.

The distribution of this book without permission is a theft of the author's intellectual property. If you would like permission to use material from the book (other than for review purposes), please contact support@lmbpn.com. Thank you for your support of the author's rights.

LMBPN Publishing
PMB 196, 2540 South Maryland Pkwy
Las Vegas, NV 89109

First US edition, October 2018

BOOKS BY SIENNA LAWSON

School of Magic

The Principal Is Missing (1)

Principal For A Week (2) - Coming soon

www.ingramcontent.com/pod-product-compliance
Lightning Source LLC
Chambersburg PA
CBHW031127080526
44587CB00011B/1144